ALL
YOU
NEED
IS LESS

VICKI VRINT

ALL YOU NEED IS LESS

An Hachette UK Company
www.hachette.co.uk

Vie Books, an imprint of Summersdale Publishers Ltd
Part of Octopus Publishing Group Limited
Carmelite House
50 Victoria Embankment
LONDON
EC4Y 0DZ
UK

www.summersdale.com

Printed and bound in the Czech Republic

ISBN: 978-1-78685-766-8

Substantial discounts on bulk quantities of Summersdale books are available to corporations, professional associations and other organizations. For details contact general enquiries: telephone: +44 (0) 1243 771107 or email: enquiries@summersdale.com.

Contents

4 Introduction:
The Power of Less

7 Less Worry

31 Less Clutter

53 Less Junk Food

71 Fewer Stressful Relationships

89 Less Input

107 Less Toxic Thinking

125 Do Less

143 Less Indoors

156 Conclusion

INTRODUCTION: THE POWER OF LESS

There are many things we would like more of in our lives: more free time; more space; a more healthy lifestyle; more positive relationships... but when our days are packed full of commitments, it can be tricky to work out how to achieve these things, let alone how to fit them into our busy schedules.

The answer is simple: all you need is less. Every area of our lives can benefit from streamlining; when you cut out the things you don't need, you leave room for the positive and beneficial things that you want to focus on. Declutter your home, for example, and you'll have space to find the things you need and store the things you love.

The same principle can help you to strip away the unhealthy elements of your diet and replace them with nutritious alternatives, or to identify the niggles in your relationships and put them behind you. By learning to prioritize and pare things down you'll feel the benefits across all areas of your life – you'll feel less stressed and more fulfilled. And it's easy to do, too, if you take it one step at a time. This book shows you how to do just that, so read on and tune in to the power of less.

WORRY OFTEN
GIVES A SMALL
THING A BIG
SHADOW.

Swedish proverb

Less Worry

It's natural for us to worry about things now and then, but if these worries spiral out of control, they can lead to stress and depression, as well as raised blood pressure and poor sleep. The good news is that you needn't be at the mercy of your worries. While all the tips in this book will help you to lead a simpler, less stressful life, this chapter includes specific ways to overcome your worries and relax. Whether you're losing sleep over an upcoming job interview or fretting over a tricky decision, take action now to send your worries packing.

I NEVER
WORRY ABOUT
ACTION,
BUT ONLY ABOUT
INACTION.

WINSTON CHURCHILL

TARGET YOUR WORRIES

The first step in tackling your worries is working out what they are. Keep a notebook handy and jot down the things that prey on your mind throughout the week. Now, take action wherever possible!

If you're worrying about a specific situation – like an exam – plan, prepare and then relax knowing that you're doing all you can. If your commute to work stresses you out, look at ways to change it. If it's a tricky relationship that's worrying you, take steps to improve matters or cut your ties (see "Fewer Stressful Relationships"). To tackle more general anxiety, see page 28.

MEDITATION

When we're feeling stressed it's all too easy to go into fight-or-flight mode – our heart starts pumping and our thoughts start racing. Meditation is the best way to stop worries in their tracks and still your mind. It's a skill that can be developed easily – there are countless online tutorials to get you started – but you can benefit straight away by simply finding a quiet space, sitting with your eyes closed and focusing on your breathing. Try the following exercise for a gentle introduction to the relaxing world of meditation and include it in your daily routine whenever you can.

Triangle meditation

1   Sit comfortably, close your eyes and relax.

2   Breathe in slowly to a count of three, hold your breath for another three counts, then exhale for three counts before starting again. (This is known as triangle breathing.)

3   Clear your mind and focus only on your breathing. (You can picture a triangle as you do this, if you like, mentally moving your focus along each side as you breathe.)

4   If your thoughts intrude, set them aside and refocus on your breathing. With practice this will get easier.

5   When you're ready to stop, gradually return your awareness to the world around you.

A safe haven

Meditation gives you a safe space to enter whenever you wish. Guided meditations – audio recordings that take your imagination on a journey – are a lovely way of unwinding. Alternatively, create your own imaginary safe haven when meditating by picturing a cosy location that appeals to you, such as a cottage fireside or a quiet corner in a library. Imagine yourself entering your haven and observe the textures, colours and smells as you look around, adding details each time you visit. Engaging your senses in this way will immediately help you de-stress, and you can return whenever you like.

LIGHTEN THE LOAD

A chat with a friend can be enough to lay your worries to rest; your pal may be able to offer an alternative point of view or help you to see the funny side of a situation. Writing down your worries can be very cathartic too. Start a journal and write in it daily – but don't forget to also write down the positives about your day. Make a note of three things you're grateful for, for example, or describe an incident that made you smile. It can really put things in perspective.

Some people
go to priests,
others to poetry.
I to my friends.

VIRGINIA WOOLF

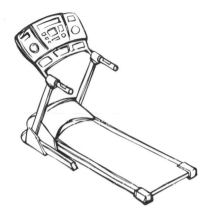

GET ACTIVE

Physical exercise is an effective way to de-stress quickly as it releases endorphins (feel-good chemicals that naturally leave you feeling calmer). Even better, you'll improve your fitness level at the same time. There are so many options to choose from: a group activity is a fun way to work out and meet new people, but if you'd rather go it alone, try running, swimming or hitting the gym. As long as you get your heart pumping your worries will soon fade. (It's hard to stress about your job when you're trying to remember the right moves in karate or Zumba!)

Make it mindful

Most of our worries arise when we dwell on past experiences or start to stress about what the future might bring. The most effective way of beating these worries is to concentrate on the present moment, and that's where mindfulness comes in. By focusing on the details of where you are and what you're doing right now, you can remind yourself that there's no need to be anxious: you're safe and everything in this moment is fine.

Mindfulness is easy to practise and you can do it anywhere. Try some of these simple mindful activities:

Mindful **listening**

Close your eyes and focus on the sounds
you can hear around you right now.

Mindful **observation**

Pick an object and focus on its shape, form
and colour, noticing the tiny details.

Mindful **conversation**

Focus fully on what is being said to you –
this will improve your relationships as
well as your mindfulness practice!

Mindful **housework**

Pick a daily task and do it in a mindful way,
engaging all your senses and working purposefully
as you do the dishes, for example.

Mindful **creativity**

Choose a hobby that completely absorbs you –
such as painting or reading – and focus on it fully.

RATIONALIZE
AND BE
REALISTIC

If you let your worries take control they can get blown up out of proportion, so ask yourself whether your worry is realistic, or whether it's something that may never materialize. If it's pretty unlikely to happen, focus on the present instead and decide that you'll cross that bridge if it (ever) comes to it. And what's the worst thing that can happen if your worry *does* come to pass? Reassure yourself that – if you did happen to lose your job, for example – you'd cope somehow. It might even be the start of something new and better.

SLOW IT DOWN

If your mind or heart is racing, learning to relax by practising some simple yoga is a good way to slow things down. Try a beginners' class or check out a few easy poses yourself, such as "child's pose", "corpse pose" or lying with your legs raised against a wall. (Practise these on waking or just before bed.) If yoga isn't your thing, Pilates or t'ai chi may appeal to you. Or try simply stretching, breathing deeply and having a good yawn to increase the oxygen levels in your blood and help to slow your heart rate.

Simple de-stressors

When you feel as though your worries are getting the better of you, there are some easy tips you can use to de-stress that trick your body into relaxing. They work every time, so are useful to know.

Simply **breathe out slowly once**, counting to 12 as you do so, and you'll instantly feel calmer. (This works because it balances the amount of carbon dioxide in the blood, which gets out of kilter when we become anxious and snatch too many breaths.) What could be easier than that?

And did you know that **relaxing your jaw** can make you feel less stressed straightaway? Our jaw muscles are the strongest in the body and we often clench them without realizing it. Try opening and closing your mouth a few times now, then let your mouth hang open and gently massage the muscles just below the cheekbones. You'll feel the tension melt away immediately.

Another easy stress-reliever is to gently **massage the web of skin between your thumb and forefinger**, which is a useful acupressure point.

DRAG YOUR THOUGHTS AWAY FROM YOUR TROUBLES...

BY THE EARS, BY THE HEELS, OR ANY OTHER WAY YOU CAN MANAGE IT.

MARK TWAIN

INSTANT MOOD-BOOSTERS

Go for a walk. Get some fresh
air and appreciate nature.

Laugh! Watch a clip of your favourite TV show
or have a chat with your funniest friend.

Play a game. Children know best!
Immerse yourself in something
fun, if only for five minutes.

Sing along to an upbeat tune or, even
better, dance around the room to it.

Be more cat! Cats know how to relax.
Have a good stretch and flex and
clench your paws... I mean hands!

Repeat a mantra. "This too will pass"
is a good maxim to focus on.

DON'T DWELL ON DECISIONS

It may be that the only way to move on from a worrying situation is to make a decision... but perhaps that decision is the biggest cause of your angst. Should you leave your job and set up on your own? Should you end a difficult relationship? We can often spend months or even years deliberating these things – and worrying the whole time that we do so.

It's common to procrastinate. We tell ourselves we don't want to rush into things, but often, deep down, we know the path that we want to take. It's taking that first step that's tricky.

Trust your instinct, bite the bullet and decide. Commit to your plan and take action. You'll feel much better for having made a move.

If you genuinely don't feel the time is right to move forward, count that as a decision too, rather than mulling things over every day. Jot down a summary of the issue and your thoughts, add a note to your calendar to revisit them in, say, six months' time, and then firmly put your worries aside. Go out, distract yourself and chances are things will have changed when you come back to revisit your problem.

Distract yourself

If there really is nothing you can do to sort your worry, distract yourself from it instead. Pick something so absorbing that your mind can't focus on anything else. If you're stumped for ideas, think about what you loved to do as a child. Why not get back to star-gazing, playing a musical instrument or practising your favourite sport? Alternatively, how about volunteering? Chatting to people who are housebound, or working with those who are struggling with life's challenges, will help you to focus on something different and help others too.

LET GO OF CONTROL!

There are some things in life we can control... and others that we just can't: you can leave for work on time, but you can't prevent the traffic jam that keeps you gridlocked for half an hour. Many worries stem from us trying to control the random challenges that life throws our way, but when you accept that this is impossible, you'll worry a lot less. Tell yourself that you can't control these challenges, but you can control the way you react to them – and remember, your success rate for getting through tricky days so far is 100 per cent.

HEALTHY BODY, HEALTHY MIND

If you're constantly feeling worried and uneasy, and can't link your worries to a specific cause, tackle your anxiety by making sure you're looking after your physical health first. Limit or cut out caffeine, nicotine and alcohol – all of which affect your mood – and eat regularly and properly (avoiding sugary foods that can cause blood sugar dips). Remember to get enough sleep and exercise too. Boost your mood by meeting up with friends regularly and give the relaxation techniques in this book a try.

If these steps don't help, you may be suffering from a stress-related condition, such as generalized anxiety disorder, social anxiety disorder or post-traumatic stress disorder (PTSD). (It's estimated that 15 per cent of us suffer from these conditions at some point or other, so you're certainly not alone.) Make an appointment with your doctor, who can advise you on the best way to keep your worries in check. All of these conditions are treatable. Cognitive behavioural therapy, which simply involves talking through your current issues with a trained professional (as opposed to analyzing the past), is often very effective.

THERE IS NO
GREATNESS
WHERE
THERE IS NOT
SIMPLICITY,
GOODNESS,
AND TRUTH.

Leo Tolstoy

Less Clutter

Today we have access to so much *stuff*. We can snap up bargains on eBay and order items for delivery the same day... and before we know it our homes are filled with clutter. But instead of making us feel happy, all these unnecessary items can have a detrimental effect on our mood. A clutter-free home, on the other hand, is a calm and happy haven. Follow these tips to streamline your living space and you'll feel much more relaxed and have more time to spend enjoying yourself, instead of stressing about the dusting!

**CLUTTER IS NOT
JUST THE STUFF
ON YOUR FLOOR –**
IT'S ANYTHING THAT
STANDS BETWEEN YOU
AND THE LIFE YOU
WANT TO BE LIVING.

PETER WALSH

STREAMLINE YOUR LIFE

Think of decluttering your home as therapy, rather than a tedious task. You'll be amazed at how it boosts your mood and encourages you to go on and achieve in other areas of life. Go through your possessions one group at a time (clothes; books; toiletries; etc.), put everything in a heap and sort out the things you really need or love. Keep these and then rehome everything else. (This is a great skill to learn – it helps you to prioritize in other areas of your life too.)

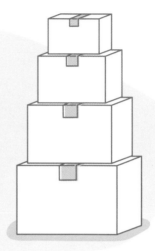

DON'T
BE A
HOARDER

When you're sorting through your possessions, be realistic about what you need to keep. Don't be tempted to hang on to things "just in case" you need them one day; they'll just end up gathering dust. (Remember you can always borrow or hire seldom-used gadgets, power tools, extra crockery, etc., if you need them at some point in the future.)

Here are some common items that people tend to hold on to when they really don't need to do so. Search these out and recycle or rehome them for a clutter-free living space:

User guides. Most appliances are easy to use and instructions can always be found online, so recycle these.

Clothes that don't fit. Ditch them and create space for the more flattering items that you *do* wear.

Old mobile phones, chargers, leads. You may have a drawer full of these because you don't know where to recycle them, so check online for your nearest recycling point.

Back issues of magazines. Pass these on as soon as you've read them, don't pile them up in the corner. (You won't refer back to them and they'll just gather dust.)

Have nothing in
your house that you
do not know to be
useful, or believe to
be beautiful.

WILLIAM
MORRIS

Pesky paperwork

Paperwork is another thing that piles up in our homes. Stem the flow by switching to paperless banking and billing. And don't add to the paper pile-up by picking up leaflets when you're out and about.

When it comes to household papers, keep copies of family certificates (birth, death, marriage); exam certificates; health/social security documents; passport and ID cards; pension documents; wills; and house and vehicle ownership papers. Keep insurance documents for as long as they're valid, and work and tax documents for seven years. (You need only keep payslips for one year, though.) If you're hanging on to anything else, get shredding!

SNEAKY STORAGE

Decluttering isn't about throwing away everything you own. Smart storage solutions can ensure that your home stays clutter-free and easy to clean. These needn't be expensive: boxes or crates are cheap to buy and can be stacked or tucked away in corners. Make use of "wasted" space under beds or on top of wardrobes by storing out-of-season clothes or craft supplies there. (Even the space under sofas can be used as a storage zone.) Check out Pinterest for some sneaky storage inspiration, or try some of the following:

A **hanging shoe rack** on the back of a door can be used to store all sorts of items.

Slot **storage baskets** under shelves to max out your storage space.

Use **small boxes** in your drawers to sort and store items of the same type.

Hang your ironing board on **hooks** on the back of a door.

For organized **clothes storage**, roll your clothes in drawers.

Tension rods are your storage buddy. Use them to hang under-the-sink cleaning products; to turn an alcove into wardrobe space; or even use as dividers in cupboards and drawers for baking sheets, etc.

DO THE DECLUTTER DASH!

Decluttering sounds like a time-consuming task, and that's why we often put this sort of thing off, but never underestimate the power of a quick burst of activity. Rather than waiting for a free weekend to declutter the living room, set a timer for ten minutes and see how much you can get done right now. Start with the area that's bugging you most – the pile of magazines stacked up in front of the TV, for example. You'll be amazed at what you can achieve in a short period of time and you'll feel great for making a start.

DON'T FEEL GUILTY

Decluttering can feel like an emotional rollercoaster. You may be tempted to hold on to items because they've been given to you by friends or family, but it's best to pass unwanted gifts on to those who will enjoy them. Recognize that the gift has served its purpose as a token from your loved one. And if you find yourself building up a hoard of birthday cards, old photos or children's drawings, go through these and keep a few special mementoes in a keepsake box. You can always photograph any that you don't have room to keep.

PASS IT ON

There are lots of easy ways to rehome your decluttered belongings. Online options include eBay, Freecycle and Facebook. Local charities always appreciate donations and many collect if you have bulky items or a large number of bags to donate. For unwanted (and unopened) toiletries or food items, think of your local homeless charities, and if it's books that you need to rehome, schools and nurseries will appreciate children's books, while some coffee shops, doctors' surgeries and most charity shops will have a bookshelf that will welcome your donations.

DECLUTTER YOUR GIFTING

When it comes to buying presents, the "gifting" area of a department store is the last place you should go. Consider giving experiences or making donations to charity in someone's name, instead of items. If you can't afford a hot-air balloon trip think about tickets to a local attraction or gifts that can be used for shared experiences – a book on geo-caching or craft supplies for a friend's hobby. You could get creative yourself and put together a games- or movie-night package for a friend, a well-earned "day off" (complete with coffee voucher) for a parent you know, or a handcrafted voucher offering something simple such as afternoon tea together.

Stop! Think! Save!

If you're a real shopping addict, try these tips to take control of your spending habits.

1   Make an inventory of everything you already have and check it before you buy. (Once you see an itemized list of your clothes or kitchen gadgets you won't be visiting the shops anytime soon!)

2   When you're tempted to buy something, stop and wait. If you wait for a week (or even an hour or two) the urge may pass.

3   Think about what you could do with the money instead and transfer the same amount to your savings account for that special goal.

4   Avoid temptation at home by unsubscribing from mailing lists.

5   Avoid temptation in the shops by being aware of the cunning tricks retailers use to tempt you; these include discount offers or placing a slalom of "bargains" next to the checkout.

6   Don't pick items up unless they're on your list.

7   If you MUST buy a particular item, think ahead and make sure you have somewhere to store it, otherwise stand firm and don't make the purchase.

PICK EXPERIENCES, NOT ITEMS

If you look back at your happiest memories, chances are they will involve things you've done rather than things you've bought – an evening picnic on the beach, for example. Experiences are much more valuable than items, so rather than cluttering up your home with knick-knacks, why not save your money for a memorable activity instead: a trip to visit a relative abroad, an afternoon paintballing or a chocolate-making course with your best friends. Keep a photo of your goal in your purse as an incentive and set up a savings account so you can watch the pennies add up.

THINGS
DON'T
MATTER,
PEOPLE DO.

ROSIE THOMAS

LESS EXPENSE

When it comes to money, less expense means more funds for trips and treats, so try trimming these costs from your monthly expenditure:

Branded goods. The biggest area of waste for most of us is in our weekly grocery shop. Plan meals ahead for the week, batch cook if possible and switch branded goods for the supermarket's own versions. (For some toiletries and medicines, the supermarket version is *exactly* the same as the branded product.) You can make a huge dent in your shopping bill with a little bit of planning and flexibility.

Gym memberships. Cancelling your subscription and exercising for free is a great money saver (see pages 148–9).

Credit cards/overdraft debt, etc. Look at consolidating your debts in one place and paying them off before you even think about saving. The interest cost on your debts will outweigh the benefits of trying to put away money for a rainy day.

Magazine and media subscriptions. Which do you really use and enjoy? (Rather than subscribe, it may be cheaper to buy one-off editions of things when you have time to read/view them.) If there are several of you in the household using different media services, consider taking out a family subscription to save money.

Going greener

There's so much you can do to declutter your lifestyle as well as your home. By consuming less you're contributing to the bigger picture, benefitting the world around you too. When you buy groceries and toiletries, think about choosing items that use minimal or sustainable packaging and don't forget to take your own shopping bags.

We can also learn from the Swedish principle of *Lagom*, which shows us that happiness comes from living a simpler life and having just enough of what we need, rather than stockpiling large quantities of food and belongings.

Look at ways of saving energy, such as lowering the temperature on your thermostat or turning off lights when you're not using them. Don't leave appliances on stand-by – the cumulative effect of this can really add up – and invest in rechargeable batteries and low-energy light bulbs. Don't forget common-sense tips, such as not overfilling the kettle and popping a lid on your saucepan when boiling water. And how about saving water by turning off the tap when you're brushing your teeth or installing a water-saving flush bag in your toilet?

Remember that all the time you're using less, you're paying less too: that means more money for life's treats.

A HEALTHY
OUTSIDE
STARTS FROM
THE INSIDE.

Robert Urich

Less Junk Food

We all know that too much of the wrong type of food is bad for us, but with so much dietary advice out there, working out exactly what we *should* be eating can seem bewilderingly difficult. Never fear, the less-is-more approach is simple and super effective when it comes to food: by avoiding processed, additive-laden products and sticking to simple fresh options you can revitalize your diet and have a major positive impact on your health. Read on to learn how.

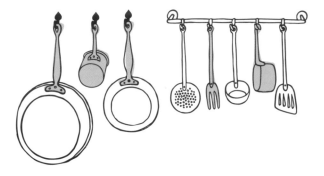

DIET DECLUTTER

A great way to start is by going through your cupboards and getting rid of unhealthy snacks and fast food options, which are all too easy to grab when you're in a rush. Restock with wholegrain rice and pasta, olives, nuts and seeds, pesto, passata and pulses to add to stews. Stock your fridge with natural yogurt, hummus, fresh salad and avocados to snack on, and dairy products, soy products and leafy greens to add calcium to your diet. Stash frozen veg and berries in the freezer and keep a well-stocked fruit bowl ready for that afternoon energy dip.

THE MORE YOU EAT, THE LESS FLAVOUR; THE LESS YOU EAT, THE MORE FLAVOUR.

CHINESE PROVERB

LESS SUGAR, MORE ENERGY

The best thing you can do to improve your health is to cut added sugar out of your diet. Sugar increases your risk of cancer, depletes nutrients in the body and is easily stored as fat. It causes your energy levels to rise and dip, leaving you feeling sluggish and craving a snack to perk yourself up again.

Chocolate, cakes and biscuits are obvious offenders, but sugar is added to everything from sauces to cereal, so check out product labels. Carbs such as bread, pasta and rice count as sugars too, but switching to wholegrain versions will help to stabilize your blood sugar level.

Saying no to sugar doesn't mean cutting out treats altogether; you just have to adapt your diet a little. Fruits such as pears, apples, plums and nectarines are a good choice (but grapes, mangoes and dried fruit are very sweet and can cause sugar "spikes"). Switch to a couple of squares of dark – rather than milk – chocolate, and swap preserves for fresh berries with a teaspoon of honey. After a week of low-sugar eating, you'll have beaten your sugar cravings and your taste buds will adapt so you'll really enjoy these healthy alternatives.

Fewer ingredients, better choice

When picking products in the supermarket, check out the list of ingredients. Ingredients are listed in order from the largest amount to the smallest, so if sugar is high up on the list try to find a healthier option (or make your own). If a product contains dozens of things, it's probably not a healthy choice, so why not stick to items with five ingredients or fewer? Choose products with ingredients that are all recognizable foodstuffs – if you don't recognize something listed, chances are it isn't good for you – and avoid artificial colourings and sweeteners.

BEATING BAD HABITS

Repeat a behaviour every day – such as unhealthy snacking – and you form a habit that's difficult to break; but remove the cue that prompts you to snack and you can tackle your habit. If walking past a certain shop means you buy a chocolate bar every day, for example, change your route to work. Or if an afternoon energy dip leads to unhealthy snacking, eat a more substantial lunch (wholegrain carbs and protein) or a piece of fruit just before you'd normally feel hungry. It can take up to two months to form new habits, but persevere and it will be worth it!

Our bodies
are our gardens to
which our wills
are gardeners.

**WILLIAM
SHAKESPEARE**

Speedy swaps

Include less of the bad and more of the good stuff with these easy swaps.

Swap a ready meal for an oven-baked
salmon steak and sweet potato fries

Swap creamy sauces for tomato-based sauces

Swap a Chinese takeaway for a stir-fry with
your favourite veggies and udon noodles

Swap pizza for pitta bread with hummus,
olives and red pepper crudités

Swap potato chips for unsweetened popcorn
or a small handful of flaked almonds

Swap fruit juice for a piece of fruit (more fibre!)

Swap sugary cereals for porridge and
berries with a drop of honey

Swap ice-cream for frozen yogurt or
Greek yogurt with fresh berries

WHAT TO CHOOSE

So what should we be eating in our junk-food-free diet? We all know that we should include at least five different portions of **fruit and veg** a day – but remember to choose as many differently coloured options as possible to max your vitamin intake.

If you eat **dairy** foods, choose three portions a day (e.g., a cup of milk, three domino-sized pieces of cheese and a portion of yogurt). Low-fat versions may contain added sugar and nasties, so use a little of the full-fat version instead. If you are vegan, pick calcium-fortified plant milk, tofu, nuts and leafy greens for your **calcium** hit.

When it comes to **starchy foods**, which should make up one-third of your diet, choose wholegrain rice, pasta and bread, or potatoes with the skins left on for added fibre.

Eat two portions of **protein** daily, such as beans, pulses, fish, eggs, lean meat or soya. And don't cut **fat** out of your diet entirely. It's great to reduce the amount of saturated fat you eat, but unsaturated fat keeps cholesterol levels healthy so include a little every day. How about half an avocado with your salad, a handful of unsalted nuts to snack on or a portion of oily fish for supper?

Shop seasonally

When you cut down on junk food and reach for the fruit and veg you'll be spoilt for choice; supermarkets can supply us with most things all year round. But buy locally produced food in season and you'll save money, help the environment and get products with more flavour too. Check online for seasonal recipe ideas and charts showing the best times to buy different fruit and veg, and look out for local box schemes that deliver seasonal produce to your door. Eating seasonally will make you feel more connected to Mother Nature, and you may even feel inspired to grow your own produce.

DRINK LESS?

Drinking too much caffeine can leave us feeling anxious and drained, so cut down to one cup in the morning and opt for decaf or herbal teas later in the day. (Green tea is low in caffeine and high in antioxidants, so it's a great alternative.)

Alcohol is a depressant (and packed with sugar), so drinking less will leave you feeling happier, healthier and less stressed. When you *do* treat yourself choose a red wine, such as Cabernet Sauvignon or Merlot, for its antioxidant properties. And one thing we shouldn't be drinking less of is water: aim for eight glasses a day.

WASTE LESS, SAVE MORE

There's nothing worse than wasting food: surveys show that the average household could save 25 per cent on its grocery spend every month by simply using up the food purchased rather than throwing it out. So...

- **Plan your week's meals ahead**, including some that will use up the same fresh ingredients.

- **Shop online** to avoid spur-of-the-moment purchases in-store.

- Check online for hacks to help you get the most out of **using your freezer**.

- Factor in a **leftovers night** and get creative with your store-cupboard staples.

And while we're talking about leftovers:

Leave leftovers from home-cooked meals to cool, loosely covered, for two hours – no longer – then refrigerate and use within two days.

Use stale bread to make breadcrumb toppings for crumbles or to coat baked fish. Or why not toast it and experiment with some creative toppings – such as fruit and Greek yogurt? You can put almost anything on a piece of toast!

Add scraps of cheese to soups or sauces and make omelettes with eggs approaching their use-by date (with other leftovers added in).

Peel and freeze bananas to make smoothies or mash up with an egg to make flour-free pancakes.

Diet detox

What you eat has a major impact on how you feel, and a diet detox will give your body a chance to reboot and leave you feeling energized. For a week, cut out wheat and white carbs, dairy, red meats, packaged foods, caffeine and sugary drinks. Go for wholegrain rice, lean protein, fruit, veg and dairy-free alternatives. It may be a bit of a challenge but you'll feel amazing for it.

(Note: If you are constantly fatigued, itchy, achy or bloated, you may have a food intolerance or allergy. Talk to your doctor – you shouldn't have to struggle on with these symptoms.)

DEJUNK YOUR TOILETRIES

It's not just the junk in our diets that we need less of...
there are additives in beauty products too. Chemicals
are easily absorbed through the skin, so why not make
your own natural treatments to avoid putting nasties
into your body? For an antioxidant face mask, mash
up half a banana with a little yogurt and honey and
apply to your face for 15 minutes. Or treat dry hair with
half an avocado mashed with a cup of mayo. (Leave
on for 20 minutes before rinsing with cool water and
shampooing.) You'll get great results, save money and
cut down your chemical footprint too.

FRIENDSHIP IS ALWAYS A SWEET RESPONSIBILITY, NEVER AN OPPORTUNITY.

Kahlil Gibran

Fewer Stressful Relationships

We interact with dozens of people each week – friends, family and work colleagues – and sometimes these interactions can get a little stressful; everyone's different, after all! But whether it's a neglected friendship that needs a little nurturing or an issue with a work colleague that needs resolution, there's always something you can do to improve your interactions and make your relationships a source of comfort, not tension.

FORGIVENESS IS NOT AN OCCASIONAL ACT,

IT IS A CONSTANT ATTITUDE.

MARTIN LUTHER KING JR

CLEARING THE AIR

Not all friendships are trouble-free: sometimes things happen and you need to clear the air to get things back on track. If you've behaved badly, apologize. If you believe the fault lies elsewhere, make the first move anyway when you are calm enough to do so. Think about what you would like to say before you meet, and make sure your friend has an opportunity to give their point of view too – but be prepared for this to be different from what you imagined! Acknowledge their feelings and see if you can find a way to move on together.

DETOX YOUR

friendship

GROUP

Our free time is precious and it's important to spend it with positive people, but some interactions can feel like more of a chore. Our friends should boost us, encourage us and make us feel valued... and we should do the same for them, of course. But if you often come back from spending time with someone feeling drained or down, it's time to take action. Trust your gut instinct: if you're dreading meeting up with someone, don't do it! Declutter your "toxic" friends and spend time instead with those who deserve you.

If you can't end a negative relationship completely – perhaps you're feeling bullied by a work colleague or put down by a family member – then do something about it. Minimize contact with the person involved and when you *do* see them set some boundaries. Tell them (calmly) how their behaviour makes you feel and that you won't be putting up with it any more. (For work situations keep a log of any negative behaviour you've experienced.) If the problem occurs again, walk away immediately and either make a complaint (at work) or cut ties with your oppressor.

Make time for loved ones

It's not always only the big things that cause stress in our relationships; sometimes day-to-day worries can put pressure on us too. This means that when we are with our significant others, we're unable to relax properly. Set aside some quality time to spend together, scheduling in a date or even a short walk in the park every week to unwind. Even better, why not try doing something new together? Whether it's learning to kayak, cook or speak a new language, it can help you see one another in a different light, away from your everyday concerns.

AVOID SECOND-HAND STRESS

Second-hand stress can be a big factor in how we feel day-to-day. If someone at work, for example, is constantly talking about what a difficult time they're having or complaining about how unhappy they are, put some distance between yourself and your stressy colleague. It's good to be supportive, of course, but don't become a sponge for someone else's negative vibes. Next time the conversation takes a downturn around the water-cooler, change the subject or make an excuse to leave rather than absorbing extra stress.

SEEING
EYE-TO-EYE

Here's something to try that will benefit any partnership or close friendship, making you feel more relaxed together and deepening your connection. It may seem a little daunting at first, but give it a go. Find a peaceful space and stand toe-to-toe with your partner, then simply look into their eyes silently for at least a minute. A few initial giggles are inevitable, but once you relax you'll find that letting someone "see" you in this way is very powerful and you'll feel equally honoured to see your partner too. It will bring you much closer together.

THE MEETING OF TWO PERSONALITIES IS LIKE THE CONTACT OF TWO CHEMICAL SUBSTANCES:

IF THERE IS ANY REACTION, BOTH ARE TRANSFORMED.

CARL JUNG

Getting closure

There's nothing more frustrating than an unresolved problem in a relationship. If talking face-to-face isn't an option, here's how to get closure without the other person present.

1. Write a letter

Writing a letter is a great way of putting across your point of view. Include a statement of fact, describing the situation and how this makes you feel. Finish by saying how you would like to move forward positively. Whether you send your letter or not is up to you – you may find that simply writing it is enough to make you feel better.

2. Talk to the picture

By speaking your thoughts aloud you can vent them directly. This is a very powerful way of releasing difficult emotions and you'll immediately feel better for doing it. Find a photo of your subject and a space where you won't be disturbed. (If you don't have a picture, draw your own representation.) Look your subject in the eye, then tell them exactly how you feel about what's happened. You may feel a little silly at first, but once you get going you'll be surprised at how easy – and cathartic – it is.

TONE DOWN YOUR TEMPER

Everyone loses their temper from time to time, but if you often do so over little things, remind yourself that you can take control of your reactions and choose to behave differently. Have an action plan for when you start to see red: take a deep breath, count to ten, repeat a rhyme if you have to... all these things will give you time to act (thoughtfully), rather than react (angrily). Later, vent your feelings by running, dancing, listening to music... anything that will avoid a tempestuous explosion!

1
2
3
4
5
6
7
8
9
10

BE A BETTER LISTENER

When you're working on your friendships, it's worth thinking about whether you are being as supportive and attentive a listener as you would like to be. It's all too easy to babble on about ourselves without giving our friends time to get a word in. Or, if they're talking, we might lose concentration and start thinking about what we want to say in response. Next time you have a chat, actively listen to what your pal is saying, think about their words, and when you say something in response make sure your sentence starts with "You" and not "I"!

CELEBRATE YOUR FRIENDS

Life is busy and it can be hard to find time to see our friends, let alone appreciate them properly. Here are some tips for strengthening and celebrating your friendships.

Quality check. Think about each of your friends in turn and write down the qualities you really admire and love about them. Even better, write a note to your friend telling them why they mean such a lot to you. It will give them a huge boost and remind you of why you value your loved ones.

Send them good vibes. Before you sleep, think of your loved ones in turn, sending each person loving kindness and acceptance (even if you're having a bit of a friendship blip!). It's a positive way to end the day.

Meet up. Schedule in a regular coffee-meet; go for a walk or run together (and encourage each other to exercise!); or just invite your pals round for a games night and snacks. The reason doesn't matter – as long as you meet face-to-face you're bound to have fun.

Baggage release

In times of stress it's easy to fall back on old behaviours that don't do us justice, such as over-reacting or storming out of the room. Today's simple disagreement could – thanks to your bad experiences in the past – end up with you treating a loved one as a past "enemy". Your baggage is raising its ugly head! Try to be more self-aware and remind yourself that your loved one isn't the same person as the over-bearing ex who put you down, or the sibling who stole the glory. You'll learn a lot about yourself and improve your relationships too.

DON'T TAKE IT PERSONALLY

Don't take it to heart if people have behaved badly toward you; it's not a personal vendetta, but just a sign that they weren't able to handle things better. Issues like this are almost always about the other person, rather than you. We might never know exactly why people have behaved in a certain way, but they are motivated by their own fears and are a victim of their own weaknesses. Try to rise above these situations and don't become embroiled in analyzing why they've happened. Life is tricky enough without picking up another person's baggage!

SILENCE IS A SOURCE OF GREAT STRENGTH.

Lao Tzu

Less Input

Life in the twenty-first century is so *noisy*. From the shrill of your alarm clock to the sound of the TV, the traffic and other people's conversations, many of us spend all day listening to a constant stream of noise. And it's not just our ears that face an onslaught of input: with 24/7 access to the media and our apps, we're constantly inundated with information and rarely have time to process our thoughts. It can be difficult to detach from all this and unwind. Quiet time is essential for our mental health, so here's how to live a life with less input.

In the midst of movement and chaos, keep stillness inside of you.

DEEPAK CHOPRA

QUIET HOUR

Embrace silence. Many of us drown out our thoughts with background noise, so turn off the radio, TV and your laptop and phone notifications for an hour every day. The best time to do this is in the evening, before bed, as this will give your mind some time to go over the events of the day and relax before you sleep. Sitting silently may feel awkward at first, so if you're struggling try a non-tech-based hobby: journaling can be very stress-relieving (see page 13) or try a few basic meditation exercises (see pages 10–11) or some gentle yoga.

SHUSH!

Turn down the volume on your day with these simple tips.

Breakfast outside (if you can) away from TV or computer screens and the radio. That way you'll start the day in tune with your own thoughts, rather than with a head full of other people's news and chatter.

Turn off the radio when driving, and try **running without headphones** – listen to the sounds of nature instead. Or **go for a walk without your phone**. Concentrate on your surroundings; you might spot something new.

Say no to the notifications that bombard you throughout the day. Switch off all but the most essential and unsubscribe from sales emails.

Focus on your breathing for 5 minutes before getting out of bed and before going to sleep. Let your thoughts flow freely.

When talking to others make it a rule to **listen first, then speak later**. Try to avoid interrupting and speaking over other people. Bring an attitude of calm to your conversations and they will be much more positive.

Tune in to birdsong

We often take birdsong for granted, but listening to it will instantly make you feel more relaxed; just find a seat outside, close your eyes and tune in. But why not go a step further and learn to identify the birds you hear? Your local wildlife group will run a course on identifying the common birds in your patch, but it's easy enough to check out their calls online. (Or, if the birds are having an off-day, the sound of the wind in the trees or a trickling stream is super-relaxing too.)

BRING AWARENESS TO THE MANY SUBTLE SOUNDS OF NATURE: THE RUSTLING OF LEAVES IN THE WIND, RAINDROPS FALLING, THE HUMMING OF AN INSECT, THE FIRST BIRDSONG AT DAWN.

ECKHART TOLLE

GET READING

How often have you bemoaned the fact that you don't have enough time to read? Well, why not use your silent time to catch up on some of those books you've been stockpiling. If you're not sure what to read, joining a local reading group will give you some inspiration, a deadline and the chance to chat about books with new people. Or you can always set yourself your own reading challenge – how about reading the top ten classics or a book from every genre at your local bookshop or library?

GET WRITING

If reading a book isn't enough, why not have a go at writing one? Writing is very therapeutic and if you turn off any distractions you can express your own thoughts rather than listening to everybody else's. Start by jotting down a paragraph or two each day. The important thing at first is to get into the habit of writing – even if it's just a review of the meal you just ate or a description of your commute! You'll soon find it becomes easier with practice; why not try a short story, a poem or that long-dreamed-about novel?

Tune out the negatives

We have access to news channels 24/7 and, let's face it, most of the stories they report are not cheery. While it's good to stay informed, try to limit the amount of time you are exposed to tales of doom and gloom, particularly in the evening when you're trying to unwind. You're not likely to get a good night's sleep if the last thing you saw before bed were the details of the latest natural or man-made disaster! Make your bedroom clutter-free and news-free – a haven to relax in before you drop off to sleep.

FEEL
THE BEAT

If you're going to listen to something, make it count! Choose a relaxation podcast or try a sound bathing session and benefit from focusing on some pure, positive sound. (Sound bathing is a type of meditation where you listen to the sound of a gong or Tibetan bowls being played.) Alternatively, why not try making your own music? Meditative drumming is a rewarding practice that produces relaxing alpha waves in the brain. Find a comfortable quiet space, and drum a slow regular beat, focusing solely on the sound of the drum and the feel of your hand lifting and striking the skin. Set aside any intrusive thoughts and you'll finish each session feeling rejuvenated and recharged.

THE POWER OF SILENCE

As you become more comfortable with silence, you will discover that it is a powerful tool to use in interactions with others. Many people find silence in conversations uncomfortable and can rush to fill it by blurting something out. But remaining silent when you don't have anything important to say, or when you're faced with someone trying to start a negative discussion, shows great strength of character and can help to keep the peace. In a confrontation simply say your piece quietly and calmly, and then use silence to show your strength.

In an interview, if you answer questions succinctly and don't ramble on to fill the silence you will come across as confident and self-assured. And don't forget to use short silences (i.e. pauses) when speaking in public; they'll give a much more polished result.

Use silence to improve your listening skills – you can learn a lot by paying attention to *how* others speak, as well as by focusing on what they say. Anyone you are speaking to will feel valued and more positive toward you if you give them the gift of a silent, attentive listener.

**SOLITUDE
HAS ITS OWN**
VERY STRANGE
BEAUTY TO IT.

LIV TYLER

Take yourself on a date

Spending time alone can be seen in a negative light and we can feel pressured into spending every spare moment socializing with others but studies have shown that regularly spending time alone makes you less stressed, more compassionate, more creative and mentally stronger too. So have a date with yourself once in a while: you could go out for a quiet coffee and take along your favourite book; go for a walk along the beach (and spend as long as you like photographing the waves) or visit a local gallery or museum.

FORGET TO CHECK YOUR NEWSFEED

— + X

Whatever your favourite social media, chances are you're spending way too much time checking it out – an average of four hours a day according to recent research. Yes, it's a great way of staying in touch with your friends – but checking Facebook for "likes" every 5 minutes or poring over pics of your pal's perfect home on Instagram can leave you feeling like a bit of a failure... and do you really want to spend 25 per cent of your day online? Switch off your device and organize a face-to-face meet up with someone who will lift your spirits instead.

− + X

Most of us dream of the things we would do if we had more time – well, four hours a day sounds like a lot of time! You could use that time to work toward a personal goal, even if it's in small bursts. If you've always wanted to travel, why not download a language app and practise that every time you feel the urge to reach for your phone. Or, if your dream is to get fitter, make a rule that you have to do ten squats before you check your newsfeed.

ALL WE ARE IS
THE RESULT OF
ALL WE HAVE
THOUGHT.

Buddha

Less Toxic Thinking

We all experience negative thinking at one time or another – no-one feels positive all the time – but a passing doubt can turn into a thinking habit, that can turn into a false belief about our abilities and have a major negative impact on our life and our decision-making. With a little work, you can stop these toxic thoughts in their tracks and turn your life around, leaving more time for positive thoughts. This will boost your confidence and leave you feeling happier and more relaxed.

OVERCOME "IMPOSTER SYNDROME"

We are our own worst critics, unfortunately, and many of us often think of ourselves as inadequate or worry that we're a "fraud" – a common condition known as imposter syndrome. Sufferers are highly critical of themselves and believe that luck – rather than hard work – is the reason for their achievements. So next time your inner critic whispers in your ear, recognize these false beliefs for what they are and remind yourself that you're doing brilliantly. It's your hard work – not luck – that has led to your achievements and you should be proud of them.

BEAT YOUR
SOCIAL FEARS

In tricky social situations it can be easy to feel that everyone's eyes are on you. When you walk into a room or have to speak in front of others you may feel that people are judging you negatively, but this is an example of you projecting your fears onto those around you. (Beware: assuming that you know what others think of you is a direct path to toxic thinking.) Stop, breathe and reframe the situation. Remember, everyone will have their own concerns foremost in their minds – they won't be thinking about whether or not you stumble. So rethink... and relax.

Rewire your brain

Many of our toxic thoughts are a hangover from our survival instincts, such as always expecting the worst-case scenario ("I'll never pass my exam", for example). But if we repeatedly think this way, we build neural pathways in the brain that make us more inclined to think that way again. The good news is that you can "re-programme" yourself to think positively. Next time you have a negative thought, write a positive affirmation – such as "I'm well prepared and organized" – to counter it. Positive affirmations are powerful tools: repeat them every day and your brain will automatically follow these new thought paths.

Jealousy is another negative emotion that has its roots in our prehistoric survival instincts. It's natural to feel envious of others now and then, but if these feelings get out of control they can be very unpleasant. Try to avoid comparing yourself to others – you are unique and wonderful, you know – but if you do feel the green mist descend, think about what is *really* bothering you and do something positive to feel better. If you're envious of someone's new job, perhaps it's time you started following your own dream. See jealousy as a sign that you need to invest some time in yourself... and do it now.

We don't see
things as they are,
we see things
as we are.

ANAÏS NIN

PICK POSITIVE WORDS

We can't control what life throws at us, but we can control how we react to those challenges... and how we speak about them too. If you always describe situations in negative terms, you've effectively made up your mind that things will end badly. Rephrase the way you refer to things – try calling a tricky situation a "challenge" rather than a "disaster", for example – and you'll develop a brighter attitude to life and find that positive results are a much more likely outcome.

HOW TO
FORGIVE SOMEONE

Anger and blame are unpleasant emotions to carry around, so learn to forgive and move on with a lighter emotional load.

Think objectively about the incident that upset you; try to see it from the other person's point of view. It's likely that they won't have meant to hurt you – perhaps thoughtlessness or a lack of courage caused the problem? Now think about your own part in the situation: have you been playing the victim? Or dwelling on things and creating more stress? Write your thoughts down in your journal to clarify them.

Now close your eyes and focus on breathing slowly and deeply. Imagine your negative feelings flowing out of you every time you exhale. (You can visualize this by seeing your feelings as a cloud of coloured energy.) Finish your meditation by saying "I forgive you" aloud, as many times as you feel necessary. If you repeat this exercise over a few days you'll feel a little better each time. And remember that forgiving someone doesn't mean you are condoning bad behaviour; it means that you're choosing to move on from it and leave it behind.

Stop complaining!

Don't waste energy moaning about the things that get you down – it will only make you feel worse and spread negative feelings. (A quick rant to get something out of your system is fine; telling your colleagues every morning that you hate your landlord is not!) Ditch the negative remarks and put your energy into fixing the situation instead. And try not to get drawn into gossiping about others; make a decision to radiate kindness, acceptance and good humour, and you'll be spreading positive vibes rather than a toxic aura.

MAKE FRIENDS WITH FAILURE

The one thing people regret in life is not pursuing their dreams. And what is it that most often stops them from doing this? Fear of failure. As schoolchildren we are taught that failure is a bad thing, but in reality failure is one of the most valuable experiences we can have. It highlights exactly what we need to do to succeed so don't let it put you off pursuing your dreams. Go for it, embrace failure when it happens and learn from the experience.

DON'T DWELL ON THE PAST

If you find yourself talking about all the things you *should've* done, or how things *could've* worked out differently, you may be living in the past and letting difficult experiences control the present and your future. Make peace with the past by writing down what has happened to you. Summarize the lessons you've learned and then pour all your energy into planning a new goal for the future. Now take a step toward that goal today, however small that step might be.

Write yourself a letter

Self-criticism damages self-esteem and impacts on your mood, so treat yourself the way you would treat a loved one: kindly, not harshly. If you're battling negative thoughts, writing yourself a letter can be very healing. Write as a trusted friend and express empathy. Explain that you understand you've done the best you can in the circumstances and forgive yourself for any perceived mistakes. Finish by telling yourself that you know you will be happy and confident again in the future.

DON'T STRIVE FOR PERFECTION

We see images every day on social media and in the world at large of other people's seemingly perfect homes, bodies and careers – but these aren't realistic images and you absolutely don't need to achieve perfection to be happy. (If you think you do, you'll be setting yourself up for a fall.) Putting pressure on yourself to look a particular way or to get five things done before breakfast is never going to end well, so ditch the to-do list (see page 137) and focus on living life to the full from the inside, not trying to style your life to appear perfect to others.

HAVE NO FEAR OF PERFECTION

– YOU'LL NEVER REACH IT.

SALVADOR DALÍ

PICK POSITIVE PRINCIPLES AND PRIORITIES

Once you've had an emotional and mental clearout and ditched all those toxic thoughts and thinking habits, it's a great opportunity to put some positive things in their place. You're already thinking positively (see page 110), but how about making a list of your principles and priorities and thinking about these as you move forward? A great rule to follow is to "behave like the person you'd like to be". So what principles would you like to live by? A good starting point is to consider who your heroes are.

Make a list of the people you've always admired – celebrities or everyday folk – and write down what you admire about them. You may find they share a common trait, which is bound to be something you value too. If you've done the exercise on page 84 you might want to include some of these characteristics too. This can help you construct your principles list. (See page 134 for how to work out your priorities.) Pin your lists up somewhere you can see them every day and use them as inspiration as you move forward in your less-stressful life.

DO LESS;
OBSERVE MORE;
ENJOY MOST.

Magda Gerber

Do Less

Many of us spend our days endlessly rushing from one thing to the next. Our job and family commitments take up most of our time and when we cram in some regular exercise, housework and time for our hobbies and friends, life becomes so hectic that we never have time to stop and enjoy it all. So *do less*... and make sure that the things you *do* devote your time to are the important ones; then you can give them your all and enjoy them to the max.

FOR EVERY MINUTE SPENT IN ORGANIZING,
AN HOUR IS EARNED.

BENJAMIN FRANKLIN

GET ORGANIZED!

The best way to gain time is to get organized and sorting out your morning routine is a great place to start. If you struggle to leave the house on time, lay your clothes out the night before and make sure your keys, bag and shoes are easy to grab before you go. (Rearrange your hallway storage if necessary.) Every weekend, plan the week ahead and make sure you have any extras you need to hand – birthday presents and an outfit for a party, for example. Less panic and stress means more time to relax and enjoy the week.

BE MORE EFFICIENT

Challenge yourself to find more efficient ways of doing the things you simply have to do every week, and you'll be amazed at the time you can save. Set up regular payments from your bank to pay bills and minimize admin. Cut down on tidying time by putting things away as you use them, and make every trip upstairs or downstairs count: what can you take with you now to save an extra trip later? If you have kids, see if you can buddy up with other parents and take turns transporting them to clubs or school.

Plan meals ahead so you don't waste time on constant top-up trips to the supermarket. (Also, if you have an idea of your commitments for the week, you'll know when you can cook and when you'll need to grab something on the go.) Prepare batches of food to last you through the week (or simply make a double quantity when you can and freeze a portion to use at a later date). It's worth doing your shopping online too – you'll save time and won't be tempted to add too many end-of-aisle treats to your basket!

Learn to delegate

Many people find it tricky to delegate, but struggling on under a heavy workload (at home or at work) leads to stress and means you won't be performing at your best either. It's your responsibility to ask for help, and chances are those around you will be pleased to give it. If you're swamped with chores at home, delegate something to another member of the household (or swap your most disliked chore for one of theirs). At work, talk to your boss or your colleagues about how best to improve your workload or streamline time-consuming tasks.

PRACTISE SAYING "NO"

It can be hard to say no when we're asked to do things, and because of this many of us end up overcommitted. Next time you're asked to take on something you don't want to do, say "I'm sorry, I can't", without feeling the need to explain. (Saying no now means that you're saying yes to having more time to pursue the things that really matter to you.) If you need time to think about someone's request, say that you'll get back to them rather than blurting out a "yes". They'll appreciate you giving the matter proper consideration.

DON'T FLIT – FOCUS!

If you try to do too much at once you'll never get anything done properly. It's much better to focus all your attention on one task and get that finished before moving on to the next thing on your list. Concentrating on one thing is also a great mindfulness exercise, so focus all your senses on your task and you'll feel calmer too. (Multitasking only works well if you can leave something unattended – such as the kettle – and do something simple while you're waiting. See how many dishes you can put away before it boils, for example.)

If you want to live a happy life, tie it to a goal, not to people or things.

ALBERT EINSTEIN

Prioritize your priorities!

What are the top four priorities in your life? Try listing them... and then deleting any that relate to work and relationships/ family (the things that take up most of your time). Does that knock out most of your list? So, now try listing your *next* four priorities and you should find yourself coming up with the interests that you're passionate about: hobbies, sports, creative pursuits or volunteering. These are the things that really make your heart sing – and if they're important enough to make it onto your list, they're important enough to declutter your schedule for.

To make time for your priorities, take a look at how you spend your week. Are there any wasted slots of time you could make better use of? If you're regularly doing things that underwhelm you, it's time to make some changes. Obviously, there are some things that we all just have to get on with – household chores, for example – but if you find yourself dreading your weekly exercise class, for instance, why not try something different that might fit into your schedule more easily, such as running or cycling. (See page 74 if it's a meet-up with a "friend" that you're dreading.)

IDENTIFY A GOAL AND SCHEDULE IT IN

Having a single, specific goal in mind can act as a great motivator for cutting out extraneous tasks (and lost minutes surfing the net). What do you *really* want to achieve in life? Perhaps you've always wanted to study creative writing or learn another language? Remind yourself of why your project is important to you and then go for it. Check out the time-saving tips in this chapter and then find an hour a week to devote to your dream. Put it on your calendar and make your dream a reality.

DITCH THE TO-DO LIST

Just how useful is a to-do list? Well, writing one can make you feel pretty efficient at first, but if you start the day with a list as long as your arm and finish it with one that's even longer, it can actually end up making you feel stressed... and like a bit of a failure. So instead of that "things I'll beat myself up for not doing today" list, why not pick just one task you want to achieve and celebrate when you get that done. You'll feel much more positive and victorious!

OUR LIFE IS FRITTERED AWAY BY DETAIL.

SIMPLIFY, SIMPLIFY.

HENRY DAVID THOREAU

Less browsing

The downside of social media is that it can be so distracting. With notifications going off on your phone every 5 minutes or with your Facebook page set as the home page on your laptop, it's all too easy to lose hours to browsing across the course of the week. Delete apps from your laptop and try to minimize the time you spend checking your phone. Check your emails in a couple of batches throughout the day, rather than as and when they arrive, and you'll find yourself with more precious time to devote to the real world.

TAKE AN EXERCISE HIIT

Exercise is important, so surely we should be doing more of it, not less? Well, studies have shown that short bursts of intense exercise (known as HIIT) are a more effective way to get fit. HIIT exercises can be done at home easily, saving a trip to the gym. If you're toning muscle, save time by using a slightly heavier weight and doing fewer reps (until your muscle is exhausted), for exactly the same results as more reps with a lighter weight. (You should obviously use your common sense and not try to lift anything too heavy, though!)

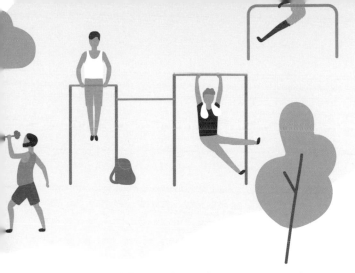

Here's a simple HIIT cardio session to keep your heart and body in shape. (Aim to do this three times a week when possible.)

- Jog on the spot until warm
- 1 minute of squats, then a 30-second break
- 1 minute of star jumps, then a 30-second break
- 1 minute of static sprinting, then a 30-second break
- 1 minute of star jumps, then a 30-second break
- 1 minute of squats
- Stretch to cool down

THE BEST
REMEDY FOR
THOSE WHO
ARE AFRAID,
LONELY OR
UNHAPPY IS TO
GO OUTSIDE.

Anne Frank

Less Indoors

Spending less time indoors and more time outside is good for you on so many levels. It lowers your stress levels and blood pressure; it strengthens your immune system and makes you fitter; it gives you time to gather your thoughts, away from the distractions of everyday life; and can even help you to feel more grounded and balanced. So what are you waiting for? There's an abundance of ways you can strengthen your connection with the natural world around you. Here are just a few.

TUNE IN TO THE SEASONS

Tucked away in our homes or workplaces, travelling by car... life in the twenty-first century can be very disconnected from the natural rhythms of the seasons; but we are wild creatures at heart and designed to be in tune with nature's cycle. Reconnect by picking a favourite beauty spot and visiting it every month throughout the year. Sit quietly and study the scenery around you: the plants, the weather, the wildlife you spot. Note seasonal changes, take photos (or a sketchbook if you're feeling really creative) and make a montage of your pictures.

THE GOAL OF LIFE
IS TO MAKE YOUR
HEARTBEAT MATCH
THE BEAT OF THE
UNIVERSE,
TO MATCH YOUR NATURE
WITH NATURE.

JOSEPH CAMPBELL

RECONNECT WITH NATURE

Spending time out and about in nature is so easy to do, and – even better – it's free. Here are five simple, rewarding things you can do to engage with the wild world on your doorstep.

Find some grass and lie on it. Whether it's your lawn or the park or a meadow, enjoy the feeling of being relaxed and grounded with the earth at your back.

While you're there, why not **cloud watch**? Slow your breathing, relax and let your thoughts drift along with the clouds.

Engage with a favourite tree. Stroke the bark; hug it if you like. Think about the age and beauty of this incredible life-form, which grew from such small beginnings.

Sleep out under the stars. Forget the tent and spend the night outdoors under the canopy of the night's sky. You might even spot a shooting star.

Helping out. Wherever you live there will be a conservation group that could benefit from your time. Whether it's maintaining local meadowland or helping at a wildlife shelter, you can give Mother Nature a helping hand.

EXERCISE OUTSIDE!

Save money on classes and exercise outside instead. It's free, you'll be working out in the fresh air and you can do it any time. Running is a great way to start – if you're a beginner try short, gentle sessions of jogging with recovery walks in between. Walking and cycling are also great options. You could do your HIIT training outside too, of course (see pages 140–1), or take a kettlebell out into the backyard and do some toning exercises there.

A park workout can be fun – go with a friend if you're feeling shy. Warm up by jogging, then mix in some sprinting between lampposts, or take a skipping rope and get your heart pumping. A park bench is useful for step-ups or tricep dips, and there are lots of exercises you can do in pairs. Try doing squat jumps opposite one another with a "high ten" at the top of every jump, or loop a towel around your partner's waist and get them to jog along pulling you behind for added resistance – don't forget to swap over!

In the spring,
at the end of the
day, you should
smell like dirt.

MARGARET
ATWOOD

WILD ENCOUNTERS

One of the best things about being outdoors
is engaging with wildlife, and any of the activities
in this chapter will bring you into contact with the
creatures that inhabit your area. Birdwatching is a great
activity; most local wildlife groups offer introductory
classes, but you can try it for free by taking a walk with
a birdspotting guidebook. Or why not help out on an
eco-project, volunteer at an animal refuge or offer
to walk a neighbour's dog? Anything that involves
interacting with animals is a great de-stressor
and has great benefits for your health.

GROW YOUR OWN

There's nothing more satisfying than harvesting your own crops. Planting things takes a bit of graft, but the exercise is good for you and it gets you outside in the fresh air. Even better, gardening puts you in touch with the seasons and the turning of the earth, helping to put your worries about everyday life into context. Whether you get your first allotment, a bed of strawberries in the backyard or just a couple of potted herbs to keep on your windowsill, you can be sure that there'll be at least one keen gardener among your friends or family who can give you some helpful tips to get started.

There is a huge variety of courses available to teach you how to cultivate your own produce or enjoy the great outdoors. You can try everything from foraging for edible plants to seasonal cookery courses, growing your own herbal remedies, tree identification and outdoor survival experiences. You could even learn to weave wicker baskets or plant a rockery. A quick internet search is all it takes to find a practical course that interests you – and maybe even discover skills you never knew you had. (If attending a class doesn't appeal, look for online courses or YouTube tutorials on your chosen topic.)

PROMISE ME YOU
WILL NOT SPEND SO
MUCH TIME TREADING
WATER AND TRYING
TO KEEP YOUR HEAD
ABOVE THE WAVES
THAT YOU FORGET,
TRULY FORGET,
HOW MUCH YOU HAVE
ALWAYS LOVED TO SWIM.

TYLER KNOTT GREGSON

GET WET

If there's one sure-fire way of experiencing nature, it's to get wet in it! Go walking or running in the rain; once you stop trying to keep yourself dry and go with the flow you will feel a great sense of freedom. Jump (for joy) in puddles. Paddle in the sea or splash through a stream. If you're feeling really bold, why not give wild swimming a try? There are lots of secluded locations where you can shed your clothes and engage fully with the elements. (Less is more, after all!)

CONCLUSION

The principle of "less is more" is such a powerful one, and I hope that this book has helped you to put it into practice so that you can start to experience the wonderful benefits of a simplified life.

Although decluttering can take a little work to begin with – whether it's clearing your garage or overhauling your calendar – remember that once you've done it you'll have a new, easy-to-maintain system in place and there will be no going back.

Now all you need to do is maintain your boundaries and stay focused on your goals; don't start taking on new commitments to fill the time you've set aside to follow your dreams! Just sit back and savour a life with less clutter and stress, and all the benefits that this will bring: happiness, peace and more time to spend doing what matters to you.

You deserve all of these things. Enjoy them!

Image credits

If you're interested in finding out more about our books, find us on Facebook at **Summersdale Publishers** and follow us on Twitter at **@Summersdale**.

www.summersdale.com